Online Income: How to use your Copywriting skills to make Loads of Money with an SMS Campaign

By Larry O'Connor

Contents

Introduction 3
    Traditional Communication 6
    How Language was used in the past 10
    How SMS came to be 13
    How our brain processes SMS 17
    What is SMS 21
    What is Natural Language 25
    How do they Differ in Regards to Usage 28
    Age and Usage 32
    Comparison of Changes 35
    No Nutritional Value 38
    Planning your SMS Marketing Campaign 41
    Setting up Your SMS Campaign 46
    Final Thoughts 49

Introduction

As copywriters we get asked to work on all kinds of campaigns. Some of them are traditional types of campaigns such as sales letters, direct sales, and sales pages. There is a new form of marketing that is becoming a major method of marketing and that is SMS marketing.

This is a relatively untapped field for the copywriter since much of what is involved does not include what we as copywriters normally do.

I'm going to show you how you can take advantage of this as a legitimate market as a copywriter and show you why it's important for you to at least be familiar with it since the involvement of consumers and their phones is reaching unheard of heights.

For example, did you know:

- Over **50%** of smartphone users <u>grab their phone</u> as the first thing they do in the morning
- 80% of Internet users own a smartphone
- 71% believe mobile marketing is core to their success
- **Mobile offers** are redeemed **10x** more than print offers

What does that mean for you?

It means you can create content that is immediately going to show the result of your campaign efforts. In short, it means more money for you for less effort. You'll create the content and a Social Media Manager will handle all the technical stuff.

There are only 160 characters in a text message and there are specific things you need to make sure of in each one. And why
160 characters? You'll find out inside but rest assured, there isn't any more needed than that.

So if you create a campaign that takes you 15 minutes and charge $100's of dollars to set it up...you are making bank as they say.

Just think, you are marketing yourself as a SMS marketing copywriter and doing one campaign after another. You'll keep getting faster and knowing what works and what doesn't.

Each one brings you closer and closer to creating that level of advertising that Claude Hopkins called an "exact science," One where's there's no worry of investment. It's that sure.

People will be coming to you and asking how you're making all this money and you will be able to coach them. At that point, your fees go even higher because if you're a coach.... you can easily charge thousands of dollars for your expertise.

And to think...all of this because you took that one step and did your first SMS campaign for your client.

Now, why would you want to do this besides the fact that the first thing half the people do is to pick up their phone after they wake up?

Well here's some reasons...

- Estimates say that mobile transactions will account for 50% of all digital spent
- 83% of B2B marketers say mobile apps are important to content marketing
- Every **text message**, according to statistics, is opened **within 3 minutes**.
- And the kicker, 97% of Americans use it every day

So why wait? Start today and get involved in SMS marketing and add it to your repertoire. Here's some of what will be covered.

- Chapter 1: I breakdown the difference between natural communication and SMS and how it's changed

- Chapter 2: I define SMS language and show how we process the messages different and why we do so
- Chapter 3: We learn the difference between SMS and traditional language
- Chapter 4: This gives us a way to look at how SMS fits into the traditional copywriting and marketing campaigns
- Chapter 5: Here we learn how to plan and implement our SMS campaigns based on the information given in previous sections
-

So without further delay, let's move into Chapter 1.

Purpose of Communication

Traditional Communication

This is a book about communicating. It's about communicating with your customers via SMS. So, I wanted to start this book off specifically talking about communication. Communication is one of the most important things we do in life. People have died without communication, they've gone crazy without it. They've done any number of things because of to much of it or not enough.

Communication is part of every life on the planet.

I love to sit in the mall and observe people and this is one of the things I like to do when I go there. I go to watch the people.

I enjoy watching them communicate Well, what they consider communication. It often goes something like this,

"*Hey Joe,*" Bob says.

"*Hey Bob,*" replied Joe.

"*How's it going, Bob*?" Bob didn't hear because Bob was thinking about what his wife told him this morning.
"*What…what??*" He asked Joe.

At this point in the conversation, Bob is not involved in the conversation at all. There is a missing element to the conversation and that is that communication is a 2-way street. It doesn't just flow one way…it flows both ways. And if one direction of the street isn't moving, then the whole thing is blocked. You will have a traffic jam and often people don't even know why.

Communication is the imparting or exchanging of information and ideas between multiple people. Another word for it is interpersonal communication. What does this mean? It means that for communication to take place, there is an exchange of dialog or ideas. It works the same way in advertising.

In fact, if you look at the *Advertising Standards Bureau,* they use the terms, "advertising" and "marketing communication" interchangeably as one and the same thing. An ad is a communication between you and your customers or clients.

Their part of the communication is how or if they respond. If they respond you know you effectively communicated. If they didn't, you know you communicated as well. You didn't communicate in a way that resonated with them. Basically, they didn't get it.

In fact, if you want to consider any advertisement or marketing program you develop or begin, you must look at it as a communication…well, actually…an interaction, if you want to be assess it correctly. You must assess it for what it is….it is communication in the form of an interaction. I'll explain that in more detail in a minute.

We don't want to look at advertising in the wrong way. If we look at it incorrectly then we cannot calculate our results correctly. That's why some consider it evil and manipulative in that it can get people to do whatever it wants them to do. But when you put it in the correct perspective you will find that those responses are a thermostat of what effect your advertising is having.

This is similar to the argument people have about guns as being evil. Now wherever you stand on the issue is irrelevant here. What I am trying to point out is that words themselves are not evil, they are just words. It is how we use them that defines them.

We must assess our communications that we use, in print, web, and SMS by the same standards we do in communication. What kind of interactions are we having? The idea of communication is that communication is what we said above, it's a facilitation between 2 or more people.

However, when we move into an interaction, we are having an influence on another party. That is the goal of our ads and our marketing. We are looking to cause some sort of interaction.

A "mutual" action...or "inter" action between two or more sources.

I find it interesting that when I was first setting up my business practice as a copywriter, I was calling our marketing programs,
"*interactions*." I hadn't really looked up the word but to say that an interaction causes an action on the other person's part made total sense then.

So let's be consistent in our definitions, we should define what each of the words mean that we use in our daily work as copywriters. We use the words: communication, interaction, conversation, and discussion.

A *communication* is: a specific form of communication that usually involves the use of language and information is exchanged.

An *interaction* is: any process that causes an influence on another party to the interaction. This doesn't have to be only related to humans as this term is used across many sciences.

A *conversation* is: A specific form of communication in which natural language is exchanged in the form of language.

A *discussion* is: a form of conversation where they not only exchange information, but they do so with the explicit intent to convince the other party of their opinion.

In our conversations and discussions about our chosen craft we should use the terms that apply in the correct way with the situation we are referring to. This will ensure accurate understanding of results and expectancy of what should or should not happen in each situation.

If I'm referring to a sales letter where the goal is clearly to get you to buy my soap, then I would not call that a conversation or communication. I would call it an interaction since I am interacting with you to influence you to do so. If I was communicating or conversing about my soap then I may be telling you how I love my soap or how it stinks so bad I can't stand to get in the shower and use it.

Years ago I was in school training to be a Paralegal. I was always very successful in any English class I took because it was an easy subject for me as it was all through my years of schooling. However, when I entered this school, I found that I missed a lot of stuff when reading statutes and case law.

I didn't realize that our brain fills in a lot of blanks and it does so with data that we have entered into it throughout our life. It will find something that fits and uses it. It's almost like predictive text on a phone. I basically told my family that I had to relearn to read since we were basically learning a new language.

Throughout this book I will be talking about different types of communications and I want to be able to communicate the correct one to you and you to be able to do likewise.

Therefore, I think it's important that we have the definitions of our field and the words we use out there in the forefront so we know and understand what each other's talking about. This way we can assess our results when we talk about our interactions with our customers.

In the next chapter we'll look at how words have been used in the past and how they are different now

How Language was used in the past

Traditionally language was something that was an art form. It was used to paint images with words that would allow a reader to be taken to someplace foreign and exotic or experience an epic battle. It even made it possible to take part in a romance that was part of history and they would never get to see. It's a paint brush without paints. A photo without a camera. In short, words were what we needed to convey our meanings to others and allowed us to share our life with them.

In fact, before the 1900's writers were paid by the word. They weren't paid by the book. So if you read a current book and then read one from before the 1900's you will find a lot of wordy descriptions. They would give beautiful descriptions of their surroundings which is good for us since it really allows us to visualize what life and surroundings were like back then.

This is an example of how wordy things were in the 1800's:

> *Sir, —As I scorn to act in any manner that may bring reproach upon myself and family, and hold clandestine proceedings unbecoming in any man of character,*
> *I take the liberty of distinctly avowing*
> *my love for your daughter, and humbly request your permission to pay her my addresses, as I flatter myself my family and expectances will not be found unworthy of your notice. I have some reason to imagine, that I am not altogether disagreeable to your daughter; but I assure you, honestly, that I have not as yet endeavored to win her affections, for fear it might be repugnant to a father's will.*
>   *I am, Sir,*
>   *Your most obedient servant*

He is basically saying: "*I like your daughter, I haven't started dating her but I would love your permission.*" Do you see how there is an artistic flow in the writing that isn't in our writing now? There was an elegance to it.

If you look at the writing of students in that time you will find that their words are flowing, interconnected pieces of art. They were taught something calligraphy, too. It was a class in "penmanship." You can see a beautiful example of it if you just look at the signatures on the Declaration of Independence. John Hancock's signature is almost famous for its beauty.

When you look at language, it is a form of communication. One definition says it's the *ability to acquire and use complex systems of communication*. With this definition then, language is thrown into the batch with art and math which is a recognized form of communication.

Language has an interesting past too. There are two schools of thoughts on the origination of language. One group says it originates from emotions and the other side says it originates from logic and rational thought. Personally, I agree with both actually. We make many decisions based on emotion and then oftentimes we try to justify them with rationality and logic.

So, in actuality, we are using both in our language. And as copywriters, we know the secret that people buy with emotions and then justify it with logic and rationality.

Still, some others simply define it as a system that allows humans to exchange verbal and symbolic utterances. This is the thought that it's a representation of an idea. This would be similar to the pictographic languages that existed thousands of years ago. Each <u>representation</u>, represented an <u>image</u> as well as a **sound** and **meaning**.

It is in this line of thinking that SMS is seems to be heading. When we see the "LOL" we know that it means the person on the other side of the text message either found what we said as funny, or at the very least, they are smiling.

In fact, if you look at the progression of the SMS language, you will see that even that was sped up with the addition of emoticons and emojis. These are pictographic representations of what we would have typed but instead we clicked on an emoji that fit what our response was. It's a shortcut to the shortcut of SMS.

So then, language is a representation of what we are thinking, feeling, seeing, and wanting to express. It's not just a "word" as we've always thought. It has a connection to every part of our being and is connected to our emotions, fears, and thinking. If I say "elephant," you immediately think of "elephant." If I say, "dog," you think of a dog you love…or maybe one you fear.

Think about the last time you were caught off guard by someone, you probably got startled and may have made a loud screech, said some choice words, or told the person off for scaring you. You didn't think about this rationally. You did it because it was the natural verbal response of your emotions. Words were, and are, connected to your emotions.

Words can be used to make you laugh, cry, yell, tell someone off, hate someone and fall in love with someone. They are probably one of the most powerful things in the world. Words have started wars, joined kingdoms, and created causes that lasted for centuries, if not forever.

Words, as we shall see, can make you purchase something, start a new habit, or make you hate something. Here's an example of how words changed a generation of people. Most of us get up every morning and have a morning routine which includes taking a shower, using the toilet, washing our face and brushing our teeth.

Did you know that the act of brushing your teeth every morning was the result of a commercial campaign in the early 1900's by a man named Claude Hopkins? His campaign was so successful, and he had such an interaction with people, that he changed generations to come.

How SMS came to be

When cell phones came out they were not able to send text messages. It was a different time for cell phone users. Even when SMS finally was available to use and to communicate only with users on the same network the texts were free.

I remember my first phone, it was around the time of the "box" phones that had their own purse to carry them around in. These and the ones in the car were the same. It really looked like you were holding a box up to your head.

Phones were used to communicate via voice like the old phones before that..you know, the ones in your house that had a cord. People would keep buying a longer and longer cord for so they could carry it in the living room and sit on the couch since it was attached to the wall in the kitchen.

Just like all the neighbors had as well. It seemed like the only place they could put a phone in a house was in the kitchen, hanging on the wall.

Then things, changed, SMS had arrived.

SMS, meaning short message service, was taken from the work of a couple men by the name of Friedhelm Hillebrand and Bernard Ghillebaert. It was found that the "perfectly sufficient" message was actually 160 characters.

After many, many tests were done on the typewriter it was found that the perfect amount of ideas could be conveyed in that many characters or less. Therefore, it was concluded that no more were needed.

It was developed by the Franco-German Corporation in 1984. After it was developed it was modified and changed over time but never moving past that 160 characters. Never past that "perfectly sufficient" amount of characters to transmit across whatever idea was needed.

Cell phones back then were not able to send messages, and the first one-way message was never transmitted until about 10 years later in 1992. It was sent by a man named Neil Papworth. What was the first message you ask? It was, "Merry Christmas."

Here's the thing though, it was sent by computer to the phone and there couldn't be a response because phones had no keypads to type a message back. All they could do was receive the message.

This was the era of PC's coming into the main stream and hackers emerging on the scene. This was the era I lived in and I remember doing hacking in my math class. I never considered anything I did like that as hacking though, because I was just there to modify programs and see what happened.

That was the era when these various technologies came into being. Phones that could be carried in your pocket were something new and no one had anticipated it. Sometimes, I am still in awe with it.

I would interject that no one seemed to anticipate it except Gene Roddenbarry who created Star Trek since he had his characters used devices that were eerily similar to the original cell phones that came out with a flip case.

After the first message was sent it was about a year later when the first company, a Swedish company called Nokia, developed the first phone that had a keypad to send texts back and forth. The phone was a Nokia 9000i. *And we thought Apple was the first company that made an "I" phone.* I guess not.

The first text messages were only able to be exchanged between the same networks. I remember this and I ended up with a huge phone bill because of it. I had a daughter that lived across the country from me and I asked my phone company for a plan where I could text her and they set me up with an unlimited plan.

Apparently they didn't know how the networks worked back then either because they set me up alright, I was set up with a plan that cost me a monthly fee plus a bill of $487....twice.

I think that was the last time I ever used that company, too.

By 1999, SMS was able to be exchanged between networks so I guess I should have waited to do that plan. It was about 1998 when I went $900 plus in the whole on an unlimited plan that was unlimited in my dreams only.

The first keyboards were actually introduced in 1997 and that was the beginning of the Blackberry phone. So if you're a lover of Blackberries, then the birthday for your phone was around that time. Up till this point they had a keyboard but they were setup differently than the traditional keyboard you found on your typewriters.

These new ones had a physical keyboard that followed the QWERTY of the standard keyboard. This made it easier to find the keys on your phone when texting since all you had to do was know where the keys were on a computer or typewriter.

It was another 10 years before the virtual keyboards were invented around 2007. I can still remember walking around thinking how surprised I was that my phone was in my pocket and I could take call when away from my house or the cordless phone in my house. It was something I didn't think I'd see in my life.

IBM came up with the Simon which was the very first phone with a virtual keypad and this was also the year of the phone that would pretty much change everything. Can you guess it? It was the year the first iPhone came out.

Actually, this was a year for quite a few firsts in regard to phones and data usage. This was also the first year that SMS usage out did phone usage. In other words, more people sent messages than talked on their phones. SMS was truly becoming a major part of society.

It's kind of funny though, because around this time is where the jokes and comments about people posting updates about everything they were doing started. If they walked to the store, they updated about it over Twitter which uses roughly the same character limit as text messaging. If they got angry they tweeted about it and everyone knew.

We were starting to see and hear about things in social media that were originally things that we considered private.

It was a change in how we looked at everything in our lives. It was also a change in how we conducted our lives as well. I remember picking up my niece and her boyfriend and it was abnormally quiet in the back seat where they were both sitting. I looked back and they were both on their phones texting away.

What I later found out was that they were arguing. Instead of arguing like people have always done they were doing it over SMS with emphasis on points stressed by all caps. This was the equivalent to yelling in a text message.

How our brain processes SMS

Researchers are finding that reading on a digital device is works on a different part of the brain than reading from something like a newspaper or a paperback book. We tend to read differently on a screen than we do in a book. When you read on a computer screen you tend to flit around the screen and look for highlights or something that stands out.

When a reader is looking at an internet page they are scanning from one highlight to another. They'll look for headlines or something that pulls them into the page.

But what researchers at Tufts University are finding is that we read books in a linear fashion. This is scanning from left to right.

This makes sense though because if you take classes on writing for the online population, they will tell you to write in short paragraphs of maybe 2 or 3 sentences long and use headings. They say to do this because people tend to scan the page.

I find this interesting because if you look at how people read the newspaper, they will look for headlines that catch their attention and then will stop for a bit on that. In fact, in direct mail they talk about the fact that people read the headlines…they often only read the body if you have caught their eye.

It is true that when you look at a web page you will find that it's set up like a newspaper in a way. You have headlines for each article and there may be 5 or 10 on a page. In a book the only place you're going to see a title or headline is at the beginning of the chapter and nothing until the next chapter. Therefore, you would actually have more of a linear reading experience than you would on a web page or in a newspaper.

There is even a term for this, it's called a bi-literate brain. It basically refers to the fact that we read things, such as books, differently than we read a web page.

Many more researchers are looking into this field. Some are concerned that the new language, things like SMS and emojis will become their own language. If this happens, what will happen to those that have problems reading SMS and digital languages like them?

In a way, I guess it will be similar to going to a foreign country and not knowing the language. You won't be able to communicate. SMS and emojis are a global language unlike English, Spanish or French. .

This non-linear approach though could be the key in understanding how they will be processed differently than natural language. In natural language, you have grammar rules to determine how to interpret it. This is a very linear way of translating and interpreting it.

But, as said above, these new ways of communicating are not natural and they are non-linear. It's a right versus left brain kind of thing. Many will use the emojis themselves in long strings of images to portray their message. This may be better for them than the person receiving it since it's up for interpretation.

Now, if we are using more SMS which according to statistics say, in 2010 there are 200,000 text messages sent every minute. That is way faster than we can talk and communicate with in verbal form. In verbal, or natural communication, like I said in an earlier chapter, we only verbally communicate about 20% of what is communicated.

The rest of it would be things like what we see, hear, feel, or smell. In other words, the input we receive would be more non-linear and the verbal part of it would be more linear.

Text messaging then would be more of a right brain communication leaving out the linear part. It would be totally right brain communicating and therefore would be a different part of the brain than our everyday language we speak. The other thing, for the most part, it's only a written language. It's not spoken.

That would associate it more with a digital language like programming also. But remember, we are talking about a language that is used for communication on a hand-held device.

Now, I've been giving a lot of time to talking about the differences between natural language and a digital language such as text messaging and emojis. I've spent some time on recognizing how the brain may process these things differently even though they are composed of the same letters.

But there's a reason for me doing this. This book is about how a copywriter can use SMS, to their advantage and recognize how it will be processed by the person on the receiving end.

We can't expect a message to go out over SMS and expect that the brain will handle it the same as natural language because so much of what we use in natural language is absent. We have to look at age group, technical experience, and habits to recognize what the result will be.

As Claude Hopkins said in his book, *Scientific Advertising*,

> The causes and effects have been analyzed until they are well understood. The correct method of procedure have been proved and established.
> We know what is most effective, and we act on basic law. Advertising, once a gamble, has thus become, under able direction, one of the safest business ventures.

We need to be just as sure in what will happen with our advertising and the effect it will have. Only then will we be able to know if it is having the necessary effect or if we need to modify it in some way.

The Difference between Natural and Text Messaging

What is SMS

So what is SMS, or text messaging? Why is it important and what does copywriting have to do with it?

SMS, or as it's known to the general public, is text messaging. You may find it called textese in reports and studies. In brief, it's a language that uses only 160 characters to convey a message. It is rather ingenious since it's brief and "enough" as its founder said, it's "perfectly sufficient."

He did some experimenting with his typewriter and found that most groups of messages could be contained in a body of 160 characters.

It is used on mobile devices and allows for easier transport of information. Many people use it and it allows you to not be on the phone for 3 or 4 hours at a time and can be done while you're shopping or sitting watching your favorite program on television.

Some even use it when they're playing an on-line game as well. They will have a headset on barking out commands to their teammates while answering texts during the less intense parts of the battle. Personally, I leave that to the "lifers" on their because I'm just trying to survive.

Unlike traditional speech, SMS uses shortened words that are not spelled like traditional language. For example, instead of "<u>great</u>" you will see "<u>gr8</u>" since when you pronounce the words they sound the same. One just takes up less letters. Another one that is pretty common is "LOL" which means something is funny and stands for "Laugh out Loud".

SMS opens up all kinds of doors and other companies came to use it that aren't necessary just telephone companies like originally was done. When it was found that there was such a small amount of characters people have found all kinds of ways to communicate messages using these short blocks.

Maybe what was said is true, maybe the messages are "perfectly sufficient" at 160 characters.

There are also progressions in emotion in SMS. You may say "LOL" if something was amusing, if it's even more so you may say "LMAO" and if it's so funny you can't stop laughing then you may say "LMFAO". They basically mean the same thing but they are meant to be able to allow you to get your message across in one text message rather than two or more.

For those that don't know what the characters stand for in the last two they are: LMAO is "Laughing My Ass Off" and LMFAO means
"Laughing My Fat Ass Off."

SMS allowed us to start sending quick messages to someone and them receive a quick response. It was meant to make things faster and it did.

The average response time on a text is **within 3 minutes**.

That's not all though, because according to CMS Report, conversion rates on Smart Phones is up 64% compared to desktop methods. Apparently, all this speed isn't enough though, because around this time that people were beginning to use text messages you could respond with what was called a "quick text."

This was a pretyped response that you could click on and then click send. It required only 2 clicks and so was even a quicker response than a traditional text.

So when SMS was introduced, it changed a whole way of looking at writing and using words. It took words and shortened them to a form of communication that took a lot of the emotional aspect out and just left in the practical. It was a form of utility rather than beauty. It changed, "*I laughed so hard my stomach hurt.*", to "*LOL.*"

Do you see the difference in those two? One has some imagery in it and the other is empty.

I find it interesting that when I looked up related topics and researched this, that no one said there was much difference between the way language is used now versus how it was used before SMS was part of our culture. And yet, look around you at the errors in spelling and the errors in punctuation.

I have had people tell me <u>they don't even know how to use a colon</u> so they just never use them.

What about in the fact that you even see government agencies sending out materials that have spelling errors and have totally wrong words used?

Even when I was in nursing school I remember a number of teachers telling the class do not use SMS on any of your assignments. If it hasn't affected our culture then why would a teacher say that at the beginning of class…even before anything is turned in? The reason is that it allows us to get more done with less space and less time.

SMS is there to abbreviate words and make them quicker to type much the same way as using the words, "*I'll*" and "*I'm*" do. They are known as contractions. Contractions are a way to save time and the usage of extra characters to allow us to talk more like we do in real life.

Even with the similarity between SMS and contractions, they are not the same thing. They would be considered a form of contraction of a word such as "l8r" is a contraction of the word "later" but it's not the same thing as when a traditional english word is contracted.

That brings us to the next topic where we go into defining more what traditional language is versus SMS language.

What is Natural Language

I knew someone who told me about some common things you find almost everywhere but when she referred to them she used words I had never heard. I didn't know what she was referring to when she was talking to me and then I clarified with her and found it was just different words because of what life was for her in her younger days.

Back then they had kitchen stoves that were an open flame and so their frying pans would have legs to sit over the flame. This was a convenience feature but because of the way it looked, they called their frying pans, not by the term we use which is "frying pan" …they called it a "spider." It had legs that spread over the flame. It makes sense to me. This was traditional language to them.

We look at traditional language as something we can hear and respond to or ignore, depending on the situation. This is not true with people that really use the SMS type of system. I was giving my niece and her boyfriend a ride somewhere and there was a conversation between them.

Later I found out it was an argument. Normally if we are in a heated argument there is raising of voices, glaring, and tenseness you can feel in the air. When I looked back at them I didn't see any of that. They were looking at their phones and texting intensely. They were almost focused on the message, and the emotion, coming through the phone.

In natural language one of the things we listen for and react to, is inflections. An inflection is where stress is placed on the word or the ending of the sentence or somewhere in the sentence. We cannot maneuver as well where there is no stress.

It's part of the unspoken part of a conversation.

It tells us if something is a question, a statement, or what. If we don't have those it's much harder to be able to tell the meaning in it. That's what makes it so hard to tell what's the meaning behind some text messages. We don't have body language, inflection, or eye contact when we're texting so it makes it much more difficult to converse and respond correctly.

In fact, when you look into communication via traditional language you will find that it's considered normal that <u>more than 75%</u> of the communication that takes place is considered to be <u>non-verbal</u>. Non-verbal communication includes body language, facial expressions, and context (meaning what's going around us at the time of the conversation.)

Some may not have heard of the contextual part as I'm referring to it. A contextual situation would be something like me saying "hi" to a stranger in a grocery store versus me saying "hi" when I'm at a political event or if I'm collecting signatures. In the first situation I'm just walking down the street. In the second, I'm wanting you to sign my ballot, or whatever it is.

In one situation it may be easier to say hello versus another time where someone may be more apprehensive. One may be just being polite and the other could be done with ulterior motive behind it.

Language, the method we use to communicate is often thought of as just something we do without thought behind it.

In actuality though, we almost always communicate with a purpose and with a motive behind it. Even if you're just saying "hi" out of the blue. It could be simply that you want some interaction and you are pulling that person into your world to get some. This is where the resistance in sales comes from.

We recognize that this person is communicating with us in a context where there is not a motive behind it and we resist them communicating with us. Many times, the first thing we think of when someone says something to us is, "what's going on?" We then begin to assess what's going on around us.

Even if you just look at the types of communication that we mentioned above there are types where our goal is to either convince the person of our opinion or it is to get them to take an action. One thing you can look at is how for some they just want people to talk to them and so they just say, "hi." There is a need as I said above for communication with another human being.

Let's find out how they differ and what we can do with this difference in the next chapter.

But first, go to www.oconnorcopywriting.com and use the code oconnor10 to receive 10% off of your first order.

How do they Differ in Regards to Usage

Texting and traditional communication are worlds apart from each other. Both have their strengths and their weaknesses. They have better places for their uses and not so good places for their uses. The trick is to know what they are about and figure out how to take advantage of their strengths and decrease the effects of their weaknesses.

First, we will list the basic differences then work into how we can begin working with both in their proper contexts.

Language as we said above is used for many purposes. Lovers use it to communicate their love for each other and then they also use it to voice their frustration in their situation and end it. Most of the time that's how it happens but there are some that have done it over text message and even some do it via either online media or broadcast media.

Either of the methods you use other than texting though, is still traditional communication that are used to vent what you're feeling inside at the time.

As a side note, I know I keep mentioning the emotions in this book but emotions play a huge part in the field of copywriting. I would say you have to get the emotions involved but I'm sure there are some of those hard-core salesmen out there that would say they can do it some other way.

Like trying to make a simply intellectual sale.

But whether you think emotions are involved or not, if it's not when you make the sale, it will need to be involved to avoid them having buyer's remorse which can lose you that sale.

Utilizing traditional language in writing allows us to spend time describing scenes, how each emotion felt and how it affected us. It tells how we reacted to it and what the outcome was. Did we cry? Did we retaliate? Did we laugh? If we laughed, how much did we laugh? These are ways in which our everyday language affects us and either helps us or hinders us.

This is a natural thing in our lives as human beings, we learn to communicate from the time we're young children and even before we're born we're learning about our mother and learning to recognize the people around us and learning voices. In fact, language is a small part of what we learn when we're that age.

But, as far as our natural language versus SMS, we are much more acclimated to the traditional. At least until we're a certain age and then are inundated into the world of SMS. Some people were born with it as part of their culture and others entered into using it after it was invented. It just matters what your age is. That is another factor that's included in how we handle traditional language versus SMS language.

I the last couple chapters we dealt with defining what SMS, or short message service is, and we defined what traditional or natural language is and the struggle there is to define it. Both are important to us as copywriters but both have their place. Here we're going to go into some important distinctions to be aware of.

I'm going to talk about a very important difference here because I believe it's one of the most important things to remember when we're using traditional language in our practice or using SMS.

As I've pointed out, the languages are very different in their structure when compared to each other. SMS ignores virtually all of the grammar rules, all of the spelling rules, and all of the rules about spacing things out to represent the breaths taken in text. That's because SMS isn't set up that way. Natural language is set up that way, that's why it's called natural language or traditional.

SMS is specifically set up for utility. It's there for convenience. In some ways, it's like a computer language where you enter certain characters to get specific responses. In computer programming you enter the rules of what you want to the computer to print out or perform. Often though, the computer doesn't speak the language literally and it has to be translated.

If we type in our code in a computer language, like one known as Python, it comes out in Python and then needs to be compiled, or translated into the language the computer speaks.

For some, that's how SMS is. They can't understand what it is saying and it has to be translated. For others, they understand it…but only so much…because you can't put emotions, other than emojis, into the message. It's like cursive writing to some and they don't understand it.

I was so surprised when I heard my nephew and niece come home one day and talk about cursive writing. When I was in school, we learned cursive from grade school and used it all through our school years.

Now, they only take it for like a month or something like that and then they are to do all of their assignments in printing.

The claim is, the teachers wouldn't be able to read it. So, whenever they see something in cursive, they can't understand it because they were not to use it when they were in school. They are now at the end of high school and the last time they encountered cursive writing was way back in like 3rd grade. It's no wonder they can't read it and understand it.

This is one of the main reasons for us to know our target audience when we put a campaign together. We have to know what aspect of the marketing campaign they will be able to use and what will get through to them. If I was marketing and writing copy for a group of people that are 70+ I would probably not use an SMS campaign to reach them. I would find another media that would apply to that age group.

So, when we look at texting, we see that vowels are removed and some numbers are inserted to take the place of the vowels and many of the letters. This makes it small enough for to fit within the confines of the text amount allotted.

In SMS, you may abbreviate a word and in some situations, you do this by taking out the vowel. For example, when you write the word "later" in traditional writing you write it as I have done. But if you write it in SMS, you would write it, "l8r" thus eliminating other letters including the vowels.

In referring to the emotional part of a word being removed, I am referring to how SMS words are set up. When you look at the composition of a word you have hard parts and you have soft parts. For some people, the word has hard parts and soft parts. The hard parts of the word are the consonants and the soft part are the vowels. The hard letters would be the logical part of the word and the soft parts would be the part of the word that holds the emotional aspect.

By writing this way, you will see that the text message, doesn't have near as much of an emotional impact as the traditional way of writing. It doesn't have the capacity to carry the emotional and descriptive part of the language like you find with the traditional words.

Dealing with the Change in Business Communication

Age and Usage

This is an interesting part of the book because most people think that as you get to your middle ages, you don't really use SMS as much and nor do you use social media. The fact is that middle age is not really an age anymore according to different studies and is more of a frame of mind. They may use it slower than millennial who text at least 67 texts per day.

That seems a lot but when you look at the average texts the average teen sends:
- they send 3,339 texts per month.

If you break it up by gender:
- females send 4,050
- males send 2,539 texts per month.

Texting though is not just limited to young people because statistics say that over 80% of adults use SMS, it's the most common phone activity of all that people do on their phones. In fact, if you have a smart phone that number goes up to about 96% and only about 43% wanting a call over a text.

The problem I run into is I get really involved I can't text fast enough and my mind feels like a dam that's getting backed up. My thoughts move faster than my fingers do. I'm the same way on a phone though. If I get going on a phone call I I will stand up and start pacing back and forth across the floor.

You can tell how worked up I am by how fast I walk because the more I get involved, the faster I move. Eventually, I have to find a hallway or go outside because I need more space.

The other thing that I've seen a lot of guys run into that are approaching middle age is that they have a hard time texting due to the size of their fingers compared to the phone keypads. I don't have problems with it but I prefer the swipe rather than the keypad entry.

These are things to evaluate when you look at who your target audience is. Who will be getting the messages you will be sending out? Will that be a group that uses texts reliably and will they be able to respond with ease. The harder you make something, just like the more they have to click, the higher chance that people will not do it.

Each extra click moves them closer to the point where they leave the site.

I did retail merchandising and I can tell you that if you give a customer any extra steps, they will just give up because it just takes too long. Then they walk away. You have to pretty much pick it up and place it in their hands in order to get a response. We are here to get a response from people and we need to know everything about them. And if you can get the info of how fat their fingers are you need to take that into consideration also.

When you're dealing with a technology like SMS, you have to be able to know how people are using it.

This will help you know how they will use what you're marketing. Statistics show, and if you look around you can verify it, that the smart phone is being used everywhere. I've been in multiple stores and seen people with their phones out comparing prices where they are with the store down the street. We are in an age of instant information and instant gratification many think.

I call this a microwave society. We have instant food, we have the internet which means instant information, we have SMS which means instant contact, and in some countries, we have transport that moves over 200 mph. We need to have everything done yesterday.

We have instant mail which some had thought would eliminate Direct Mailings, but it hasn't. But, since we have email, unfortunately, people expect this from the marketing efforts too. It is true, though, that in an online campaign we can measure results much faster and adjust pretty quickly.

The other thing to take into consideration also is how different age groups use their smart phones. For the most part, you have a very, very small group of people who use blackberries, and a small group that uses flip phones. The majority of people are using smart phones. When doing any type of marketing you should follow the 80/20 rule and market to the 80% and expect some of the 20 percent.

You may miss a few but you are hitting the majority of the population and that's what's needed in advertising campaigns.

While it's true that the majority of the smart phone's users are people anywhere from 15 to 30, the elderly are moving up in rank and according to a Pew poll, they have moved up from 17% to 28%. The thing that happens is that usage changes.

As people get older they have issues with seeing and so they change from a small phone screen to a handheld tablet. This allows them to play games like they like to do but be able to see what's going on with it.

When I worked in tech support for Apple, it was apparent that when you see people moving into their 60's, they start getting devices like iPad's and things like those. Like I said, it has a lot to do with being able to see the screen and the variety of apps make it easy to find something that interests them.

Now, how do we pull this together into our research phase of setting up our campaign? We'll talk about that next.

Comparison of Changes

So how do we deal with all of the variety in ages we have in our society and how do they affect our marketing efforts. First, we need to know our demographics, especially in the area we're wanting to market to for our product or service.

Then we apply that to our market segment according to the technology that will be prevalent with that population.

If we know them, then we know what form or media they will be using. We need to know their habits so we can figure out our target timing. For example, if I asked you what most older folks are doing between 7 and 8 every weekday, here in the United States, you would probably say they are watching Wheel of Fortune and Jeopardy. And that would be correct. That is what most would be doing.

How about from 5 to 6? You would probably be correct in saying they would be watching the news. This is not to say this is a hard and fast rule and you need to make sure you check the statistics for the group you are working with but rest assured that they have a traditional routine they follow every day.

Statistics can sometimes catch you off guard.

I was surprised to find out that probably 70% to 80% of real estate agents are over the age of 40. Why, you ask? It is probably because when a person hits a certain age they begin to be pushed out of traditional jobs they had or they are just wanting a change in careers.

Real Estate allows them to exercise their skills they have developed over the years and to hopefully build up a nest egg for when they retire.

In every marketing, or promotional, you must understand who your reader, client, or customer is. If at all possible, you must know everything about them:

- Age
- Gender
- Occupation
- location
- Hobbies
- Marital Status
- Style of clothing
- Do they wear jewelry/personal adornments
- Any clubs they belong to
- Do they use coupons
- Religion
- Activities

All of these seem like stretching it but they are just beginning.

You notice I said location above? That is a big one because I have lived most of my life on the west coast in the Pacific Northwest but when I went to the North East, specifically, Maine, it was a difference in culture like I never expected. They were so different to everything I had seen anywhere I had been.

It was like going to a foreign country but staying on the continent. It was probably one of the top strangest things I've experienced. It felt like it was separated from the rest of the U.S.

This makes me think of another piece of data that you must include when gathering and compiling all of this data. You need to look at the general attitude of your group. Culture, age, gender, occupation and social interactions can change people's attitudes, or their reactions to others and how they view society. For example, as I spent more time in Maine I realized they were very segregated from the rest of society and they liked it that way.

For them, they looked at themselves as the first state in the United States and made sure everyone knew it. This was a source of pride for them. For example, my wife at the time was born in Maine, but since she left Maine for only about 3 or 4 years and then went back; she was considered an outsider.

And as a friendly reminder for your own safety, if you go there <u>don't mention</u> that the *first colony* in the United States was the Massachusetts Bay colony. There is a long-standing quarrel between them and Massachusetts about if that was "Mainers" or if it was the "Massachusettsans."

What about the south? They have very strong cultural ties to their way of living. They also have a very, strong religious culture for the most part also. All of these things will influence their buying decisions as well as how they will access technology. This affects all aspects of their life as well in many cases.

Now, what about wearing jewelry or personal adornments? This is also a question that could be attached to some pretty strong group associations and strong identifications with each other. For example, there are at least two religious groups I can think of off the top of my head that do not wear any jewelry. But, I'm not just talking about wearing plain old jewelry, I'm also talking about piercings and tattoos that connect them with others who do the same thing.

Fast Food Language vs Gourmet Language

No Nutritional Value

Remember earlier when I compared this to a fast food and microwave society? Well, it definitely applies to the food aspect and to the speed that people want things to be done. Our art of copywriting evolved from direct marketing and direct sales. That was the days when you would get the long sales letters that would tell you how you too could be part of the elite and sign up for your subscription to whatever product was being sold.

Now, we click on an email and have about 3 seconds to keep that readers attention and draw them into the body of the email where the sales process takes place. We then engage their emotions and let them know how our product is going to absolutely change their life when they start using it.

This is the meat and potatoes for the marketer.

In SMS marketing we don't have those parts so clearly defined. Nor do we have as much space to work our magic with the copy either. This is why I use an analogy of fast food versus gourmet.

A way to look at this process is to compare it to eating. Looking at it this way would see **SMS** communications as fast food communicating and **natural language** would be compared to a gourmet meal. One is there to engage the senses and one is simply to get some nourishment, or what is called food, into your system.

For example, fast food is there to just get something in your stomach which is why we get it and go. A nice restaurant that serves gourmet food is there to sit down and enjoy the ambiance. One of them is meant to increase our nutrients we ingest and to keep us balanced and one is simply to say we ate something.

This is a massive difference when you compare the effect one has on us and the effect the other one has on us. Whether they help us or hinder us is what's important and what we must look at. When I look at an SMS, I am looking at it to see what type of information it has, if any, and if it will be of value to me. This determines whether or not I am going to click on it or not.

Also, I check to see whether it makes sense that I'm receiving it. When I look at a book or a web page, I am at a location has a full set of values in the form of texts, images, or videos that I have been brought to either by browsing, searching, or linking.

An SMS message would be a snapshot of what's to come if I continue. It's a preview of what the meal will be like. It's like the appetizer. Oftentimes people put in a weblink for someone to click on and follow where they will get more information on what they are looking for. Our goal in SMS is to get their attention and entice them to move forward in what they are trying to accomplish. I need to paint as much of a picture as I can of what will happen if they click on that link.

Here's another way to look at it.

I arrive at the restaurant I want to eat at and I'm sitting at my table waiting for the waitstaff. I watch as everyone passes by my table and soon my waiter arrives with menus and some water. I'm asked how I'm doing and I say fine.

I am then asked if I know what I want and I reply, "I'm not sure yet."

At this point, the waiter asks me if I had thought of any appetizers and suggests the "Deep Fried Onion Rings" which are to die for. I say okay and he leaves to return with my appetizer.

When he arrives back with those I'm ready to order and I order the "Fillet Mignon" He leaves again and I enjoy my appetizer and the drink I ordered.

Then my food arrives and I finish an excellent meal that consists of an appetizer, a main course and dessert if I choose to have it.

In this analogy, my appetizer is an SMS and the meal is the sales copy that I attracted my client to. That meal will sell them on whether they will be returning and buying again. The dessert would be the P.S. in the letter or what's called the "add-on" which only ads to the bottom line.

That is our goal. To make sales, attract customers to our list, or to subscribe them to our service. We are getting them to respond to our call to action.

Copywriting Needed with New Lingo

Planning your SMS Marketing Campaign

So now we get to the whole purpose of this book. We are going to begin to set up our SMS campaign in the most efficient way so we can get the most efficient results. We/re are going to work our way from beginning to end. But first, we're going to do an overview of what will be taking place so we're all on the same page and give some preliminary things to go into as we begin this process.

There are some goals that we as copywriters and marketing professionals should already know when we get to this step.

Things we need to know include:

- What's the goal(s) of our marketing efforts
- Who are we marketing to
- What demographic is it
- Know your core segment
- Is there a time-zone difference we have to work around
- Are they going to include things like triggered messages
- Is it a front end campaign or a back-end campaign
- Do they already have a shortened URL or do you need to create one
- Is it related to a product that the customer is buying

You need to have goals about the campaign..both your goals and their goals. You should make them smart (specific, measurable, attainable, relevant and timely). You as the copywriter will probably have more experience about what is realistic when setting these also. You will know about how long it will take to complete different components of the campaign and should use your professional expertise when doing your initial session with the client.

You may be able to help them understand some things they may have missed also.

When you have a specific goal it needs to be related to the fact that you need to know who the customer is and what the customer wants to have happen. Specific goals would be things like: what is it the client wants to achieve? Where are they now compared to where they want to be? What do they consider a successful campaign?

What are acceptable losses and when do they modify aspects of it? Will they be doing an A/B test as well?

If you don't have this information how will you and the client be able to assess what is a successful campaign? This is part of the "attainable" part. Will it be something that can actually be done in the campaign you're setting up? Are they realistic or relevant? In some of these abbreviations for SMART the "R" is actually "Realistic" and not "Relevant." This may help to define what this part of the acronym refers to.

Lastly, timely refers to part of the time-frame for the campaign and also for the parts there may be in the campaign as well. This would refer to "triggers." Are they having the SMS go out at specific times with certain triggers? If so are the triggers realistic and are they applying the SMART to those as well?

All of this needs to be done since you as the copywriter will be preparing the materials that will be being used in the campaign. A social marketing specialist will be most likely handling the campaign and the process while you will be creating the materials they will use. You need to have some background in this though to know what will be needed and to be informed so you can prepare material that will be effective.

So, after this, first things first. We should have interviewed our client about the campaign and what they hope to achieve. What are the goals of the campaign and what are they hoping to gain from it. Who are they wanting to target with the campaign? Is it feasible, or able to be accomplished, according to your expertise as a copywriter? Are they using the correct technology for the group?

Before anything begins you must have it narrowed down exactly what is happening and what they are wanting to accomplish with it. This is the number one rule in any of copywriting...know your customer and know the goals of what you are wanting to have happen.

You will want to know what your demographic is and the segmentation of it. In other words, you want to know who your market or your customer is including age, gender, race, place they live and you also want to know what their traits are.

This last bit is known as <u>segmentation</u>.

If you create a campaign for someone to subscribe to a newsletter and the actual goal of the campaign is to visit a landing page, then you have created a road to something that is not going to meet your customers goals. It will be a failed project and your client will not look favorably on it.

Another thing to make sure of is whether it's related to new customers or existing customers. The former is called a frontend campaign and the latter is called a back-end campaign. A back-end campaign is meant to energize existing customers.

These questions will help you decide what types of messages and words to include in your material. It will have to do with where they will be directed also since those that are already familiar with the product will be sent somewhere with a message like "renew now" and someone new will be given a message like, "sign-up now."

If triggered messages are being used they have to be timed so that they will take place during a specific time when it will be most effective. A message that is opened within the first hour is over 50% more effective than one that is not in that time frame. To be most effective it is extremely important that you time it around the event that's it connected with. Connected with this idea of timing, remember that if some or all of the customers are in a different time zone that you will have to adjust accordingly to make sure that the messages don't arrive hours after the effective time they are meant for.

It will defeat the whole purpose if they do not arrive at the right time and could cost you the campaign.

One of the last things and probably most important is that your message should be concise and to the point. You don't have a place for frills in a text message. It's a benefit reinforced, call to action, including time-frame if applicable. The time-frame should always be included because you want them to respond as soon as possible because you don't want them to go past that 60-minute window.

You need to make sure they have a relevant keyword that will be placed in the text message and make sure it stands out. In most cases you should capitalize it to make sure it contrasts against the rest of the text and from the short code. A short code is the number they will text to.

Both should be prominent in the body of the SMS.

Sometimes the SMS is related to an activity of the receiver. It's like when you start to leave a page on the Internet and when you do a box pops up letting you know about this last-minute deal. You can click or miss out. SMS can be related to something like that and trigger an activity you want to happen.

This happens a lot on back-end marketing when a customer hasn't clicked on the app or visited the store in a while and so a SMS is generated to bring them back in with a special deal just for them for returning.

I can say from experience this is pretty effective. I have a restaurant here I shop at and if I haven't been in a while, they will send me a message with an offer that's often too good to refuse.

Next, we will go into actually setting up your SMS campaign and there is a way you can start out with it for absolutely no money.

Setting up Your SMS Campaign

Now we begin the actual setup of your SMS campaign and getting you the results you need and want. For those starting out I personally like it when someone finds a way for me to do that that is pretty much painless and simple and gives me a chance to get my feet wet and learn what I'm doing.

Well, I did do that and I found what appears to be one of the easiest places to do that. Pricing is nice too compared to what I found when looking to get pricing details for you. Originally, I found pricing that was $15-$25 a month per keyword and then a minimum of 4 to 5 cents per message sent. That could be a pretty hefty fee depending on how many texts you're planning on sending out.

I found a company that has awesome reviews, it's called EzTexting and it's found at http://www.eztexting.com. Here are some of the reviews on it. I get nothing from this recommendation but found it useful and wanted to share it with you.

> "The easiest and most cost-effective way to send messages to our admitted students. —*Creighton University*
>
> "Clear billing options, pay as you go, no monthly fees." —*Dries Jennsens, State Continuing Education*

And, there were tons more like this. The idea is that it's simple, cost effective and allows you to flawlessly begin your campaign and get moving ahead with your goals.

With eztexting.com you can use the Free and Ez plan and get 250 free SMS/month. That's right, it says FREE. And when you look in the FAQ's….it says it's really free. And then it scales based on what you do in the campaign and where you go from there.

Now, I'm taking this from the setup from their site. It's info on the how-to on setting up your first campaign with them. So, feel free to go there if you run into any problems with this.

Now, you do have an option with their service too. You can choose to do a push campaign that's designed to offer products or services to your already opted-in database or you can choose a pull campaign to build such a list. That will be a decision you will need to make as you proceed in setting everything up.

The steps are pretty simple after you choose your option from the two I talked about above.
- Create your account
- Then you want to activate it once you get the text message you're going to receive
- Then you'll create a contact group
- Next, you'll create a campaign and pick when the message(s) go out and to which group
- Then, you will send out your first text message

That, is how simple it is going to be to set up your first campaign. Then, after you do that a few times you're going to be an expert and won't need a simple way to do it.

There are some caveats, or warnings, to keep in mind when you set up your campaigns and you should always keep them in mind. These are requirements by law and you must always follow them to keep yourself safe and making money.

The first is that they have to have given permission. I found about this the hard way as I was affected by it. I was applying for a loan and filled everything thing out like I was supposed to do. It was a reputable place from everything I could find and when I was done it said I was not approved but captured a lot of my information which included my phone.

It was strange and I didn't know until later that it was just a site to capture information, such as cell phone numbers, to send you a barrage of text messages advertising other things. I had to respond to each one and text "stop" back to them to end it.

The problem was that I had never approved any of them in the first place.

All these rules must be followed to remain in compliance with the agencies that regulate SMS actions like this. They are there to protect the public. The 3 agencies are: FCC, CTIA, and the Mobile Marketing Association.

They help keep you in line with the TCPA (Telephone Consumer Protections Act) which has instituted some changes that affect companies wanting to use SMS for advertising.

There are two of these that are required at all times:

- There must be an "established business relationship"
- And "prior written express consent" cannot be a condition of a purchase.

You have to have both of them in order for it to be valid so keep that in mind. You can google ideas for how to set the language up but I found some good information at ConvinceandConvert.com that talks about it pretty clearly.

Those are the most important things to look at in setting SMS campaigns up. Remember, most messages are opened within something like 3 minutes. And, on top of that and to get you really stoked for starting your SMS marketing efforts, remember that statistics show that 50% of people grab their phones as the first thing they do when they wake up.

So with that…happy marketing to my fellow copywriters and clients.

Final Thoughts

So, there you have it. You have learned about how SMS differs from natural language and how our brain actually looks at it differently and processes it. You've seen how we communicate with each other and how this in itself is something to look at in every marketing campaign you begin. Communication, and when I say communication, I mean the way your customer communicates. Not how we communicate.

Our most important part of how successful our campaigns will be is totally based on how, not if, our reader or customers respond. Nothing else matters and there is always a response. Remember that, even if they don't respond or react to your message is exactly what I'm saying...that is your response. It's part of how they're communicating with you.

I'll say that again...every reaction from our audience...is a RESPONSE! Even if they don't buy or convert or interact; they have given you the answer of the effectiveness of your campaign and what all of the combinations involved in it equate to. If you do these exact same things, you should get the same response.

Always look at it that way. Did they respond? Okay, what was the response and was it the response we wanted?

This is how we need to look at and analyze every campaign:
- Was there a response?
- If not why?
- If there was a response, was it the result we wanted?
- If not, why?
- What parts did the campaign consist of?
- What parts can be modified to narrow down what didn't work?
- After this, what are you going to change for your next campaign?
- Repeat the analyzing we did above

Every campaign, no matter what it is has at its most basic level, 3 steps:

- Setup Campaign with applicable variables
- Watch for reaction
- Analyze reaction and response

When we do all of these steps and apply what we've learned about the different forms of communication including the way our minds and emotions react to them. Then we can begin building campaigns that will be efficient and much more effective.

We can build on old successes and eliminate failures. This is by all intents and purposes of how all direct mail campaigns were conducted. Find what works…continue to use it…find what doesn't…and drop it.

Well, that's it. Thanks for reading this. I can't wait to see you get the success you are wanting to achieve. Visit www.oconnorcopywriting.com and use the code oconnor10 to receive 10% off of your first order.

www.ingramcontent.com/pod-product-compliance
Lightning Source LLC
Chambersburg PA
CBHW071201240526
45470CB00017B/1148